Published By Adam Gilbin

@ Travis Kung

Bulletproof Diet: Gain Energy and Increase Your Health Weight Loss, Energy Boost, Bulletproof Coffee, Upgraded Diet, Well-being, Optimum Health

All Right RESERVED

ISBN 978-87-94477-61-1

TABLE OF CONTENTS

Grass Fed Sirloin Steak, Macadamia Dressing, Raw Asparagus Salad 1

Steamed Fillet Of Haddock With Fennel, Lemon & Parsley 3

Savory Avocado And Salmon 5

Potato Soup, Bulletproofed 6

Bulletproof Ceviche With Avocado And Arugula 8

Bulletproof Highfat Salad 10

Delicious Paleo Donuts 12

Sweet Potato Bacon Cakes 15

Panseared Grassfed Beef Steak With Avocado Salsa 18

Lemon Herb Wildcaught Salmon With Steamed Veggies 20

Plantain Pancakes 22

Banana And Egg Pancakes 24

And Zucchini Breakfast 26

Shakshouka 28

Thai Breakfast Scramble 31

- Brussels Sprout Hash 33
- Avodeviled Eggs 35
- Baked Burgers 37
- Spinach And Cranberry Salad 38
- Cabbage Slaw With Pomegranate And Hazelnuts 40
- Sausageburger Balls 43
- Coconutcrusted Chicken 44
- Classic Beef Stir Fry With Veggies 46
- Roasted Chestnuts With Paleo Style Coconut Macaroons 48
- Baked Coco Shrimp 51
- Tuna Salad 53
- Lamb Cumin Loaf 55
- Sockeye Salmon Dill Loaf 57
- Braised Indie Salmon 59
- Highoctane Coffee Or Tea 62
- Avodeviled Eggs 64

Moroccan Style Grass Fed Lamb With Sweet & Sour Sprouts 66

Hand Dived Steamed Scallops With Ginger And Spring Onion 68

Spanish Style Mussel And Hake Stew 69

Bulletproof Rice 71

Carrot Soup 73

Baked Rosemary Chicken Thighs With Broccoli Soup 75

Shredded Beef With Brussels Sprouts 78

Allamerican Breakfast 80

Chicken Sushi 82

The Frugal Breakfast Of Your Dreams 85

Easy Chicken Curry 88

Beef And Veggie Stirfry 91

Broccoli And Cauliflower Soup 93

Cauliflower Chowder Recipe 94

Beef Short Rib Soup 96

Smoked Salmon Frittata 98

Bread 100

Winter Vegetable Salad 102

'Whatever' Stove Top Dinner 104

Creamy Broccoli Soup 105

Lime Infused Steamed Broccoli 107

Icy Green Bulletproof Smoothie 109

Shepherd's Pie 111

Cashewginger Butternut Soup 113

Fresh Buttered Scallops 115

Creamy Tomato Soup 118

Savory Beef Bake With Zucchini 120

Perfect Parchmentbaked Salmon 122

Grilled Salmon And Zucchini 124

Baked Burgers 127

Creamy Cauliflower 128

Beef Carpaccio, Hazelnuts & Egg Yolk Dressing 130

Trout And Avocado Lettuce Wraps 132

Red Onion Squash Soup 134

Betterforyou Bulletproof Salad 136

Avocado Dressing 137

Guiltfree Ranch.. 138

Bulletproof Steak Bowl... 139

Grass Fed Sirloin Steak, Macadamia Dressing, Raw Asparagus Salad

Ingredients:

- ½ cup macadamia nuts
- 1 teaspoon fresh thyme leaves
- Juice of 1 lemon
- ½ garlic clove, minced
- 2 grass fed sirloin steaks
- 3 cups asparagus
- 6 tablespoons coconut oil
- Salt and pepper to taste

Directions:

1. Lightly heat griddle.

2. Shave asparagus with a speed peeler into ribbons and set aside in a bowl.
3. Take a small blender and add the macadamia nuts, half the coconut oil, thyme leaves and lemon juice. Roughly blend and season with salt. Set aside.
4. Rub the rest of the coconut oil over the steak and season with salt and pepper. Add to the griddle and cook to your liking. For a thick steak cook around 4 minutes each side for medium rare.
5. Once steak is cooked, take out and leave to rest. While steak is resting pour the macadamia dressing on a plate and add the raw asparagus ribbons on top.
6. Slice the steak and serve on top of the dressing and salad.

Steamed Fillet Of Haddock With Fennel, Lemon & Parsley

Ingredients:

- ¼ cup flat leaf parsley, chopped
- Juice of 2 lemons
- 3 tablespoon coconut oil
- 2 fillets of haddock
- 2 cups fennel, finely sliced
- Salt and pepper to taste

Directions:

1. Place fillets of haddock in bamboo steamer and cook for around 810 minutes.
2. Add the fennel, lemon juice, parsley and salt and pepper to a bowl with the coconut oil. Mix well.

3. Serve the salad on a plate on top of the haddock fillets.

Savory Avocado And Salmon

Ingredients:

- Wild sockeye salmon, smoked and refrigerated
- 1 avocado, sliced
- Sea salt, to taste

Directions:

1. Cut the salmon into thin, long strips and wrap around avocado slices. Serve with a dash of sea salt and enjoy!

Potato Soup, Bulletproofed

Ingredients:

- 2 tablespoons MCT oil
- 3 cups water
- Sea salt, to taste
- 2 tablespoons grassfed butter, unsalted
- 3 cups sweet potatoes, cubed
- 1 ½ cup carrots, peeled and sliced
- 1 tablespoon fresh ginger, grated

Directions:

1. Over mediumlow heat, warm the MCT oil in a large pan. Incorporate potatoes, carrots, and ginger.
2. Cook for about 2 minutes and add water. Cover the pan and simmer for about 30

minutes, or until vegetables are soft but not soggy.

3. Add in salt. Remove from heat and use a blender to achieve your desired consistency. (Skip this step for a chunkier soup.) Incorporate butter and mix well.

Bulletproof Ceviche With Avocado And Arugula

Ingredients:

- 1 teaspoon Brain Octane C8 MCT oil
- ½ avocado, cubed
- 1 scallion, thinly sliced
- 1 tablespoon cilantro, torn
- ½ cup arugula
- 8 ounces skinless, boneless wild salmon, cubed
- 2 tablespoons fresh lime juice
- 1 teaspoon extra virgin olive oil
- Sea salt

Directions:

1. Toss the salmon, oils and lime juice, then fold in avocado, scallion and cilantro. Season with sea salt.
2. Refrigerate and let sit for at least two hours. Stir occasionally to distribute the lime juice. You can marinate longer as long as you keep it refrigerated.
3. Fold in arugula before serving.

Bulletproof Highfat Salad

Ingredients:

- 4 ounces smoked wild salmon, separated into pieces
- 1/2 avocado, cubed
- Handful unroasted cashews
- 1/2 red bell pepper, sliced (optional omit if you're sensitive to nightshades)
- 2 cups wild greens mix (arugula, romaine, etc.)
- 2 pastureraised eggs, hardboiled and quartered
- 2/3 cucumber, thinly sliced

For dressing:

- 1/3 cucumber

- 3 tablespoons Brain Octane C8 MCT Oil or olive oil

- 2 tablespoons apple cider vinegar

- Fresh cilantro and oregano, to taste

- 1/2 half avocado

- Sea salt, to taste

Directions:
1. Combine all the salad Ingredients: in a large bowl.
2. Blend all the dressing Ingredients: until smooth and creamy.
3. Toss the salad in the dressing and serve.

Delicious Paleo Donuts

Ingredients:

- ½ teaspoon of vanilla extract
- 2 tablespoons of coconut oil
- 1 teaspoon of apple cider vinegar
- 2 eggs
- ¼ cup of unsweetened chocolate
- ¼ Teaspoon of baking soda
- 3 tablespoons of pure maple syrup
- ¼ teaspoon of almond extract
- 2 tablespoons of coconut oil

Directions:

1. To begin with you will have to preheat the oven to 360 degrees Fahrenheit. Grease your six mold donut pan with coconut oil.
2. After that, combine your dry Ingredients: into a medium bowl. In another bowl you should try to combine all the other Ingredients: and set up the egg whites.
3. It is now time to mix all the Ingredients: together and set them aside. Beat the egg whites until they are nice and soft.
4. Gently fold the egg whites into the batter. Equally distribute the batter between the six donut molds and smooth out the top of each donut.
5. You should bake the donuts between 12 and 15 minutes until they turn into a light golden color.
6. Allow the donuts to cool and remove them from the pan and let them chill in the refrigerator for about half an hour.

7. Place the glaze Ingredients: in a sauce pan and place the sauce pan into the skillet. Gently mix the Ingredients: until they are fully melted.
8. Pour the melted chocolate into a bowl and gently dip each chilled donut into the chocolate.

Sweet Potato Bacon Cakes

Ingredients:

- 500 grams of sweet potato
- 3 cups of flower
- ½ teaspoon of baking soda
- 2 cups of sugar
- 1 cup of butter
- 1 teaspoon of vanilla extract
- 1 teaspoon of cinnamon
- 2 teaspoons of baking powder
- 2 eggs

Directions:

1. To begin with you will have to peel your sweet potatoes and then simply place them in a hot pan and cook them.
2. It is now time to use a bowl and add three cups of flour and two cups of baking powder.
3. You will also have to add one teaspoon of cinnamon and half a teaspoon of baking soda and ¼ teaspoon of salt.
4. It is now time to thoroughly mix all of the Ingredients:. In another bowl you should add two cups of sugar and one cup of butter.
5. And mix them up. It is now time to add 1 teaspoon of vanilla extract and mix the Ingredients: really well.
6. After you mix all the Ingredients: you should add two eggs and continue to mix for a few minutes.
7. After you are done with mixing you can use another bowl to mash all of the potatoes.

8. You need to get them mashed really well and then add 2 cups of sweet potatoes to the mixture and mix it until it is nice and smooth.
9. Finally, you need to transfer the mix to your baking pan and bake at 350 degrees for 15 minutes.
10. In the end you should have your fast, delicious and easy to prepare sweet potato cake.
11. I really hope that you will enjoy this recipe as this is one of my alltime favorites.

Panseared Grassfed Beef Steak With Avocado Salsa

Ingredients:

- 1 ripe avocado, diced
- 1 small red onion, finely chopped
- 1 lime, juiced
- 2 grassfed beef steaks
- Salt and pepper to taste
- 2 tablespoons grassfed butter or ghee
- Fresh cilantro, chopped

Directions:
1. Season the steaks generously with salt and pepper.
2. Heat a large pan over mediumhigh heat, then add the butter or ghee.

3. Once the butter is melted and hot, add the steaks. Cook to your preferred level of doneness, usually about 45 minutes per side for mediumrare.
4. While the steaks are resting, combine the diced avocado, chopped red onion, lime juice, and cilantro in a bowl. Mix well.
5. Serve the steaks topped with a generous spoonful of avocado salsa.

Lemon Herb Wildcaught Salmon With Steamed Veggies

Ingredients:

- 1 garlic clove, minced
- Fresh herbs (dill, parsley, etc.), chopped
- Salt and pepper to taste
- 2 wildcaught salmon fillets
- 2 lemons, zested and juiced
- A mix of colorful veggies: broccoli, bell peppers, and carrots, for example

Directions:

1. Preheat your oven to 400°f (200°c).
2. Place the salmon fillets in a baking dish. Drizzle with lemon juice, sprinkle with lemon zest, garlic, herbs, salt, and pepper.

3. Bake for 1520 minutes, or until the salmon flakes easily with a fork.
4. While the salmon is baking, steam your vegetables until they're tendercrisp.
5. Serve the baked salmon with a side of steamed veggies.

Plantain Pancakes

Ingredients:

- 3 tbsp. of coconut oil

- 2 tsp. of vanilla extract

- ½ tsp. of baking soda

- 2 large green plantains, peeled and quartered

- 5 6 pastured egg whites

- a pinch of sea salt

Directions:

1. Peel the plantains and put them in a blender along with the rest of the Ingredients: and blend till it forms a smoothlike batter (this will take about 12 minutes).

2. Heat 1 tablespoon of coconut oil in a pan on medium heat. Then pour the batter mixture into the frying pan. Feel free to adjust the

amount of batter added at a time. Maybe you prefer lots of little pancakes over a few bigger ones.

3. Allow them to cook for 45 minutes on one side or until little bubbles form on the top.
4. Turn them over and cook on the other side for 2 to 3 minutes or until they are done.
5. Repeat steps 4+5 with the remaining batter. You can add a little extra coconut oil to the pan if needed.

Banana And Egg Pancakes

Ingredients:

- 1 banana

- Pinch of cinnamon

- 3 tbsp. Of coconut oil (i tried this before using grassfed butter instead which also worked well)

- 2 pastured eggs

- Pinch of sea salt

Directions:
1. Mash the banana in a bowl and whisk in 2 whole eggs and add a pinch of cinnamon.
2. Heat 1 tablespoon of coconutoil in one pan on medium heat. Then pour the batter into the frying pan. Feel free to adjust the amount of

batter added at a time. Maybe you prefer lots of little pancakes over a few bigger ones.
3. Spread the batter on a nonstick pan and cook like an omelette, but do not it in half. Cook pancakes till brown on both the sides.
4. Turn them over and cook on other side for 2 to 3 minutes until they are done.
5. Repeat steps 4+5 with the remaining batter. You can add a little extra coconutoil to the pan if needed.

And Zucchini Breakfast

Ingredients:

- ½ onion, finely chopped

- 1 tomato

- 1 or 2 pastured eggs

- 1 tsp. apple cider vinegar

- ½ cup zucchini, diced

- ½ cup yellow squash, diced

- 1 tbsp. ghee or grassfed butter

Directions:
1. Melt the ghee or butter in a skillet over a lowmedium heat.
2. Add the onions and cook until soft, about 6 to 7 minutes.

3. Add the yellow squash, tomato and zucchini to the skillet and season to taste. Cook for 7 to 10 minutes.
4. Whilst the vegetables are cooking bring a saucepan filled with water to a boil, and add the apple cider vinegar. This is for poaching the egg.
5. Gently crack the egg into the water and allow it to swirl around in the water until it begins to set, this takes about 12 minutes.
6. Place the vegetables in a bowl and set the eggs on top.
7. Finally, sprinkle the eggs with some extra salt and pepper, if you want, and serve.

Shakshouka

Ingredients:

- 4 cloves garlic, minced
- 1 ½ teaspoons paprika
- 1 ½ teaspoons cumin powder
- ¼ teaspoon chili powder
- Pepper to taste
- Salt to taste
- 8 pastured eggs
- 1 ½ tablespoons grass fed ghee
- 4 medium tomatoes, chopped
- 1 large onion, chopped
- 1 small green bell pepper, chopped

- 1 small red bell pepper, chopped
- 2 Serrano peppers, chopped
- 2 tablespoons cilantro, chopped

Directions:

1. Place a large skillet and place it over medium heat. Add ghee to it. When ghee melts, add onions and sauté until light brown.
2. Add garlic and Serrano pepper and sauté for a couple of minutes until fragrant. Add bell peppers and lower heat. Cook until bell peppers are soft.
3. Add spices and sauté for a few seconds until fragrant. Do not let the spices burn.
4. Add tomatoes and simmer until sauce thickens. Add salt and stir.
5. Make 8 small cavities in the sauce at different places in the skillet. Break an egg into each of the cavities.

6. Sprinkle salt and pepper. Cover and simmer until the eggs are cooked. Cook the eggs as per your desire.
7. Garnish with cilantro and serve.

Thai Breakfast Scramble

Ingredients:

- 4 small garlic cloves, minced
- 6 eggs, well beaten
- 1 teaspoon chili powder
- A large pinch freshly ground black pepper
- 2 tablespoon fresh cilantro, chopped
- 2 scallions, sliced
- 2 teaspoons fresh ginger, peeled, minced
- 4 teaspoons coconut oil or grass fed ghee
- Salt to taste

Directions:

1. Place a skillet over medium high heat. Add coconut oil. When oil is melted, add ginger, garlic, and scallions.
2. Stirfry for a few seconds until fragrant and add beaten eggs. Scramble the eggs by stirring constantly and cook until the texture you desire is achieved.
3. Sprinkle salt, chili powder, and pepper powder.
4. Add cilantro. Mix well.
5. Remove from heat and serve.

Brussels Sprout Hash

Ingredients:

- 6 grape tomatoes
- 4 eggs
- 3 teaspoons coconut oil
- 2 tablespoons grass fed butter
- Salt to taste
- 10 large Brussels sprouts, halved
- 1 onion, sliced
- 1 large sweet potato, chopped
- Pepper powder to taste

Directions:

1. Place an ovenproof skillet over medium heat. Add coconut oil and butter. When the butter

and oil melts, add sweet potatoes and onion and sauté for a while until slightly tender.
2. Add Brussels sprouts, salt and pepper and sauté for another 5 minutes. Add tomatoes and sauté for a couple of minutes.
3. Remove from heat and crack eggs over it. Sprinkle salt and pepper.
4. Place the skillet in a preheated oven and bake at 350 degree F until eggs are set to the consistency you desire.

Avodeviled Eggs

Ingredients:

- 1 T organic shallot, minced
- ½ tsp. celery seed
- Sea salt (to taste)
- 8 hardboiled eggs
- 1/2 large ripe avocado, mashed
- 1 tsp. raw apple cider vinegar
- Organic paprika (to garnish)

Directions:
1. Slice the eggs in half lengthwise and gently pop the yolks into a bowl.
2. Add the avocado, vinegar, shallot, and celery seed. Mash and mix until well combined.

3. Add salt to taste. Spoon or pipe the mixture into the egg halves and garnish with a sprinkle of paprika.

Baked Burgers

Ingredients:

- 1 t dried rosemary
- 2 t dried oregano
- Sea salt (to taste)
- 2 lbs. Ground beef (if not grassfed, use lean)
- 2 tsp. Ground turmeric
- 4 slices bacon

Directions:
1. Preheat oven to 325 degrees F. Make about 8 burgers. Combine the spices and rub them directly onto the burgers. Salt to taste.
2. Put a halfslice of bacon on top of each burger and put them on a flat baking pan with sides. Bake for 1520 minutes to desired doneness.

Spinach And Cranberry Salad

Ingredients:

- ¼ cup dried organic cranberries
- 12 tablespoons water
- 2 tablespoons organic almonds slivers
- 1 ½ tablespoons organic extra virgin coconut oil
- 2 cups organic kale, finely chopped
- 3 cups organic spinach

Directions:

1. Heat coconut oil in a frying pan. Take care that it does not get overheated.
2. Add in chopped kale with a tablespoon of water.

3. Kale has to be softened which would take about 3 to 4 minutes of cooking.
4. Once kale looks done, throw in the cranberries and again cook for 2 to 3 minutes.
5. Finally add spinach and cook it till it turns limp.
6. Toss in almond slivers and turn off the heat.

Cabbage Slaw With Pomegranate And Hazelnuts

Ingredients:

- 4 cups of organic fresh and tender spinach
- 68 radishes (red or white is optional)
- ½ cup of chopped organic hazelnuts
- A generous dash of fresh chopped coriander
- 1 organic pomegranate
- 1 teaspoon sea salt
- Organically grown purple cabbage
- 1 organic carrot
- 1 tablespoon organic fennel seeds

Directions:

1. Using a sharp knife, cut spinach very finely.

2. Thereafter cook cabbage and spinach separately for 10 and 3 minutes respectively. (It is advised never to use spinach and cabbage uncooked)
3. Then let both cool and place them in a large bowl.
4. Add a teaspoon of salt, toss spinach and cabbage. Use your fingers for the purpose and squeeze them lightly for about 1 minute making them even more tender and soft.
5. In order to cut carrots into thin strips use a potato peeler.
6. Scrape the radish and cut it into long and thin slivers.
7. Add radish and carrots to the cabbage and spinach mix and give it a toss.
8. Now take the rubies from the pomegranate, hazelnuts, and chopped coriander and fennel seeds and add them to the bowl.

9. Add salt to taste and prepare the dressing for the salad.
10. Take 1 tablespoon apple cider vinegar, 3 tablespoons extra virgin olive oil, ½ teaspoon organically prepared mustard, juice of organic pomegranate and whisk it all in a bowl.
11. Add salt to taste.
12. Place the salad on each plate and add to it a generous drizzle of the dressing.
13. Enjoy and get ready to gather all the compliments coming your way.

Sausageburger Balls

Ingredients:

- ½ lb. ground beef
- 1 egg
- ½ lb. spicy sausage or chorizo
- oregano or basil (to taste)

Directions:

1. Preheat oven to 325 degrees F. In a large bowl, mix all the ingredients. Form the mixture into bitesized minimeatballs.
2. Cook in a flat baking dish with sides until desired doneness is reached, about 1015 minutes.

Coconutcrusted Chicken

Ingredients:

- Fresh parsley
- Dried oregano
- 1 lb. chicken, cut into strips
- Shredded unsweetened coconut flakes or powder
- Sea salt
- 2 eggs

Directions:

1. Preheat oven to 325 degrees F. Mix the coconut, salt, parsley, and oregano in one bowl.
2. In another bowl, beat the eggs until well blended.

3. Dip the chicken into the egg and then roll in in the dry mix until coated. Bake until it starts to brown.

Classic Beef Stir Fry With Veggies

Ingredients:

- 2 stalks of celery, chopped finely
- 1 red bell pepper, deseeded and cut into thin strips
- ¼ cup of wine, burgundy
- 3 tbsp. of lemon juice
- dash of sea salt and pepper for taste
- 4 ounces of carrots, thinly sliced
- 1 clove of garlic, pressed
- 12 ounces of sirloin steak, trimmed, boneless and thinly sliced
- 2 tbsp. of olive oil

- 1 onion, yellow, medium in size and thinly sliced

- 4 ounces of mushrooms, thinly sliced

Directions:

1. Take a large skillet and on medium heat, add the garlic, half of the wine and a tablespoon of oil.
2. Sauté the beef for 5 to 7 minutes or until the beef starts browning. Scoop out the beef and set aside.
3. Heat some more olive oil and sauté the red pepper, celery, carrots and onion for 4 minutes or until the onion becomes tender.
4. Add the remaining wine, mushrooms and lemon juice to the skillet. Stirfry all the vegetables together for 3more minutes.
5. Add the meat and stirfry for another minute more before taking it off the heat.

Roasted Chestnuts With Paleo Style Coconut Macaroons

Ingredients:

- dash of sea salt for taste
- 1 lemon, zest only
- 1 tsp. of vanilla extract
- 1 ½ cup of coconut, grated
- 2 eggs, whites only and pastured
- 1 tsp. of vanilla
- ½ cup of honey, raw
- 2 tbsp. of coconut oil

For the coating:

- 1 tsp. of coconut oil

- 1 tbsp. of chestnuts, roasted

- 3 ½ ounces of chocolate, dark

Directions:
1. Preheat your oven at 350 degrees. While it heats up take out a baking dish and line it with some baking paper. and set aside.
2. Then using a large sized bowl, combine your honey, lemon zest, vanilla, sea salt and the egg whites together using a whisk until all of the Ingredients: are evenly mixed together.
3. Keep whisking until it becomes foamy.
4. Next add in your coconut oil and the coconut flakes into your bowl. Whisk again until thoroughly combined.
5. Set aside and let your mixture rest for about 20 minutes.
6. Then take a tablespoon and use it to tightly pack a ball of the mixture. Place your ball onto your baking sheet.

7. Continue making the balls of mixture until all of your batter has been used up.
8. Place your baking sheet into your oven and allow it to bake for about 10 to 12 minutes or until the macaroons begin to turn gold in color.
9. Remove from your oven and transfer them onto a wire rack to cool.
10. Then use a double broiler and melt your dark chocolate. Then mix it together with your coconut oil in a small sized bowl.
11. Once the coconut macaroons have cooled completely, dip one end into your chocolate while the chocolate is still piping hot. Then sprinkle some of your chestnuts on top and allow the chocolate cool.
12. Serve with a side of coconut cream and enjoy when you are ready.

Baked Coco Shrimp

Ingredients:

- 250g shrimps, peeled & deveined
- 1 cup shredded coconut
- 1 clove garlic minced with
- 3 tablespoons coconut oil

Directions:
1. Melt the coconut oil and put it on a bowl. Add the garlic to the oil and mix well.
2. Add the shrimps to the bowl and toss them to coat with the oil mixture.
3. Dredge the shrimps in shredded coconut. Press the coconut shreds onto the shrimps to make sure they stick well.
4. Arrange the shrimps on a baking sheet, put the baking sheet in the oven and bake at 350

°F for 25 minutes. Let the shrimps cool a bit before serving.

Tuna Salad

Ingredients:

- 1/2 cup freshly squeezed lemon juice
- 1 red onion, chopped finely
- 1 red bell pepper, diced
- 2 teaspoons fresh rosemary, chopped ½ cup parsley, chopped
- Pinch of salt
- 250 grams tuna fillet
- 4 cups mixed salad greens
- 1 tablespoons capers, rinse
- Pinch of pepper

Directions:

1. Place tuna in a pan, cover it with water and season it with a pinch of salt.
2. Bring the water to a boil and cook tuna for about 5 minutes.
3. Place the tuna on a plate and let it cool. Then, flake it.
4. Combine tuna, capers and onion in a bowl.
5. In a salad bowl, whisk together lemon juice, olive oil and a pinch of salt and pepper.
6. Add the mixed salad greens to the oil and lemon juice mixture and then toss to coat.
7. Add the tuna mixture to the bowl and then gently toss again to combine before serving.

Lamb Cumin Loaf

Ingredients:

- 3 tablespoons water

- 4 large pastured egg whites

- 1 pound ground lamb

- 1 teaspoon apple cider vinegar

- 1 tablespoon ground cumin

- 1 teaspoon cumin seeds

- 2 teaspoons dried oregano

- 1 leek, well washed, white and light green parts only, thinly sliced

- 1 head bok choy, stalks only, thinly sliced

- 3 medium carrots, finely chopped

- 1 teaspoon sea salt

Directions:

1. Preheat the oven to 320°F.
2. In a medium saucepan, combine the leek, bok choy, carrots, and water.
3. Cover and cook over mediumlow heat until tender, about 10 minutes. Transfer to a large bowl to cool slightly, about 5 minutes.
4. Add the egg whites, ground lamb, vinegar, ground cumin, cumin seeds, oregano, and sea salt. Mix well to combine. Form into a loaf and place in a 9 x 5 x 2inch loaf pan.
5. Bake until just cooked through, 35 to 40 minutes. Let rest in the pan for 10 minutes before slicing.

Sockeye Salmon Dill Loaf

Ingredients:

- 2 teaspoons dried dill

- 1 teaspoon sea salt

- 6 large pastured egg whites

- 1 leek, well washed, white and light green parts only, thinly sliced 2 cups chopped arugula

- 1 cup chopped fresh flatleaf parsley leaves

- 2 pounds wild sockeye salmon, cooked, chilled, and flaked into small pieces

Directions:
1. Preheat the oven to 320°F.
2. In a small skillet, cook the leek over mediumlow heat until fragrant, about 3

minutes. Transfer to a large bowl to cool slightly.
3. Add the arugula, parsley, dill, salt, and egg whites. Mix well to combine.
4. Carefully fold in the salmon. Form into a loaf and place in a 9 x 5 x 2inch loaf pan.
5. Bake until just cooked through and the egg white is set, about 50 minutes. Let cool in the pan slightly before slicing.

Braised Indie Salmon

Ingredients:

- 1 head bok choy, cored and chopped
- 4 wild sockeye salmon fillets (3 ounces each)
- 1/2 teaspoon cumin seeds
- 1/2 teaspoon fennel seeds
- 1/2 teaspoon black mustard seeds
- 1/2 teaspoon fenugreek seeds
- 1/2 teaspoon nigella seeds
- 1 teaspoon sea salt
- 1/2 cup coconut oil
- 1 leek, well washed and thinly sliced (optional)

- 2 celery stalks, thinly sliced

- 2 carrots, finely chopped

- 5 spears baby asparagus, trimmed and finely chopped 1 can (14 ounces) coconut milk, well shaken

- 1 tablespoon Bulletproof Brain Octane oil (or MCT or coconut oil)

Directions:
1. In a medium pot, combine the leek, celery, carrots, and asparagus and cook, stirring often, until softened, about 4 minutes.
2. Add the coconut milk, bok choy, salmon, cumin, fennel, mustard seeds, fenugreek, nigella seeds, and sea salt.
3. Cover and simmer until the vegetables are tender and the fish is just cooked through, about 10 minutes.

4. Plate and drizzle with the coconut oil and Brain Octane oil.

Highoctane Coffee Or Tea

Ingredients:

- 2 cups lowtoxin brewed coffee (or green tea)
- 12 T grassfed butter
- 12 T coconut oil

Directions:

1. While the coffee is brewing, put hot water in a glass blender to preheat it.
2. When you're ready to make your highoctane coffee, empty the water.
3. Put all the Ingredients: into the blender. Put the lid on with a kitchen towel over it.
4. Holding the lid down with your hand (and the towel), blend the beverage until you have a nice froth on the top. [You can use an immersion or hand blender but it won't mix as well.]

5. Pour into your mug and drink somewhat slowly to give your body time to process the oils.

Avodeviled Eggs

Ingredients:

- 8 hardboiled eggs
- 1/2 large ripe avocado, mashed
- 1 tsp. raw apple cider vinegar
- 1 T organic shallot, minced
- ½ tsp. celery seed (optional)
- Sea salt (to taste)
- Organic paprika (to garnish)

Directions:
1. Slice the eggs in half lengthwise and gently pop the yolks into a bowl.
2. Add the avocado, vinegar, shallot, and celery seed. Mash and mix until well combined.

3. Add salt to taste. Spoon or pipe the mixture into the egg halves and garnish with a sprinkle of paprika.

Moroccan Style Grass Fed Lamb With Sweet & Sour Sprouts

Ingredients:

- Thumb sized piece of ginger, minced
- 2 tablespoons Moroccan 7 spice.
- 2 cups, Brussel sprouts, halved
- Juice of 1 lemon
- 2 table spoon honey
- 1 ½ pounds grass fed lamb shoulder, boned
- 1 onion, diced
- 2 clove garlic, minced
- Salt and pepper to taste

Directions:

1. Add the lamb, onion, ginger, garlic and 7 spice to the slow cooker and cook on low heat for 6 hours.
2. Once the lamb is cooked, pull apart with a fork and set aside.
3. Lightly boil the Brussel sprouts in water with and drain. Toss with the honey, lemon juice and salt and pepper.
4. Serve alongside the lamb. Drizzle the honey and lemon juices around the plate.

Hand Dived Steamed Scallops With Ginger And Spring Onion

Ingredients:

- ¼ cup spring onions, sliced thinly
- Juice of 1 lime
- 2 table spoon coconut oil
- 68 hand dived scallops
- 1 tablespoon fresh ginger, sliced thinly
- Sea salt to taste

Directions:
1. Place scallops in bamboo steamer with the ginger on top and cook for around 4 minutes.
2. To serve garnish with spring onions and pour the lime juice and coconut oil on top.

Spanish Style Mussel And Hake Stew

Ingredients:

- 3 clove garlic, diced

- 1 tablespoon pimenton

- 1 teaspoon saffron

- ½ cup parsley

- Juice of 1 lemon

- 4 tablespoon virgin olive oil

- 2 large fillets of Hake, cut into squares

- 1 pound hand dived mussels

- 2 onions, diced

- 5 cups fish broth

Directions:

1. In a deep frying pan, start by lightly frying the onion and garlic in the olive oil.
2. Add the pimenton and cook for a further 4 minutes.
3. Add the fish broth and saffron and bring to boil.
4. Lower the heat and place the Hake in carefully.
5. Add the lid and cook on a low heat for around 10 minutes.
6. Remove the lid and add the mussels, close the lid and cook for a further 4 minutes.
7. To serve, garnish with the parsley and a squeeze of lemon.

Bulletproof Rice

Ingredients:

- 12 tablespoons MCT oil
- ½ lemon, sliced
- 4 tablespoons ghee, divided
- 2 cups white rice, cooked
- 2 lemons, freshly squeezed
- Sea salt to taste, if desired

Directions:
1. In a large saucepan, heat 2 tablespoons of the ghee on mediumlow.
2. Add in cooked rice and combine thoroughly. If desired, add a dash of salt, and pour in about ¾ of the freshly squeezed lemon juice.

3. Stir frequently and cook for up to five minutes, or until Ingredients: are hot.
4. Add in the remaining butter and stir for one more minute. Remove from heat and top with remaining lemon juice and garnish with lemon slice.

Carrot Soup

Ingredients:

- 2 fennel bulbs, finely chopped
- 2 inches fresh ginger, chopped
- 4 cups water
- 2 tablespoons MCT oil
- 2 pounds of carrots, chopped
- 2 celery stalks, finely chopped
- 2 tablespoons grassfed butter, unsalted

Directions:

1. Heat carrots, fennel, and celery in a large pot on medium. Incorporate celery and ginger and cook until Ingredients: have softened and are wellmixed. Add water and stir thoroughly.

2. Cover and allow to cook on medium for up to one hour, but no less than 40 minutes.
3. If desired, remove from heat and use a blender to create a smooth consistency. Add butter and combine thoroughly.

Baked Rosemary Chicken Thighs With Broccoli Soup

Ingredients:

- 2 sprigs of fresh rosemary
- 1 teaspoon smoked paprika
- Sea salt
- 2 bonein, skinon, pastureraised chicken thighs
- 1 tablespoon Brain Octane C8 MCT Oil

For broccoli soup:

- 1 head broccoli
- 3 tablespoons grassfed butter
- 1 teaspoon sea salt

Directions:

1. Preheat oven to 350 degrees F.

2. Pull the skin away from the meat of the chicken thighs so it's separated, but still attached. Slip a sprig of rosemary between the meat and skin. This will infuse the meat with flavor and ensure that the skin crisps.
3. Rub the Brain Octane oil on the outside of the chicken thighs, then sprinkle with smoked paprika and sea salt.
4. Put the chicken thighs on a baking sheet. Bake until no longer pink and juices run clear, about 30 minutes.
5. While the chicken is baking, cut the stalk off the broccoli and set it aside.
6. Boil or steam the broccoli head until tender, about six minutes.
7. Blend the broccoli, butter, sea salt and 2 tablespoons of the water from the pot until smooth. Add more water if the soup is too thick.

8. Plate the chicken and put the soup in a bowl. Serve together.

Shredded Beef With Brussels Sprouts

Ingredients:

- 2 tablespoons Brain Octane C8 MCT Oil
- 3 tablespoons grassfed, unsalted butter
- 1 1/2 tablespoons apple cider vinegar
- 1 pound grassfed bottom sirloin or skirt steak
- 2 tablespoons sea salt
- 1 tablespoon ground turmeric
- 1 teaspoon dried oregano

For Brussels sprouts:

- 2 teaspoons sea salt
- 2 teaspoons ground turmeric
- 1 pound Brussels sprouts (halved)

- 2 tablespoons grassfed, unsalted butter

Directions:
1. Coat the steak with the salt, turmeric and oregano.
2. Place the seasoned steak in the slow cooker and pour on the Brain Octane C8 MCT Oil. Add the butter and cook on low for six to eight hours, or until the meat is shreddable. After the meat is cooked, shred it with a fork and add the vinegar.
3. To make the Brussels sprouts: Preheat the oven to 300 degrees F. Place the sprouts in a baking pan with the butter.
4. Sprinkle on the salt and turmeric. Bake for 30 to 45 minutes.
5. Serve beef with Brussels sprouts and enjoy.

Allamerican Breakfast

Ingredients:

- 1 tablespoon grassfed butter or ghee
- 1 avocado, sliced
- 4 slices pastureraised bacon
- 4 pastureraised eggs
- Sea salt

Directions:

1. Pan fry the bacon over medium heat until cooked but not charred, about four minutes each side. Set aside, and reserve the bacon fat for a later meal.
2. Clean the pan and return to medium heat. Add butter, then eggs. Fry the eggs until the white cooks.

3. Tilt the pan so the butter pools. Spoon the butter over the eggs until the white on the top cooks.
4. Plate the eggs, sliced avocado and bacon. Add sea salt to taste and serve.

Chicken Sushi

Ingredients:

- 1 sheet of nori

- 50 ml of vinegar

- 50 grams of sliced cucumber

- 100 grams of boiled rice

- 50 ml of sesame seed oil

- 200 grams of chicken

- 30 ml of sweet teriyaki sauce

- 50 grans if sesame seeds

Directions:

1. In order to fry the chicken you need to mix it with some hot sesame oil. You will want your chicken to be cooked but not over cooked

because if you overcook the chicken it will be very dry. Finally you need to flip the chicken and add some teriyaki sauce.
2. It is now time to set the chicken aside and start rolling a bamboo rolling mat. You will have to place a sheet of nori on top of the bamboo mat.
3. You will now take the sushi rice and you will spread it out evenly over your nori sheet.
4. Flip the rice sheet over and place two pieces of chicken along with some sliced cucumber.
5. Finally, you will have to roll the bamboo sheet and compress it. In the end you will have to cut the sushi roles in thin pieces.
6. The ideal width should be of about 1 inch. Anyway it is now time to get the sushi and add it on your plate.
7. If you want to give your sushi roles a really special taste you can try to add just a little bit of ginger.

8. You should drizzle some teriyaki sauce over the sushi roles and this will give your sushi roles a really glossy and sweet honey like aspect.
9. In the end you can sprinkle some freshly roasted sesame seeds on top of the sushi roles.

The Frugal Breakfast Of Your Dreams

Ingredients:

- 200 grams of bacon

- 250 grams of brie

- 10 eggs

- 250 grams of hash browns

- 30 grams of butter

Directions:

1. The first thing that you need to do is to cook your bacon. While your bacon is cooking you can prepare your eggs inside of your muffin pan.
2. You need to stir your eggs inside of the muffin hole. When the bacon is done cooking move it to the side and let it to cool down.

3. I would recommend cooking your eggs in your bacon grease because they will taste better and they will be crispier as well.
4. You should make sure to cut your bacon into really small pieces. It is now time to sprinkle a little bit of bacon onto the eggs that you have in your muffin holes.
5. The last thing that you are going to add is your brie cheese. You should make sure to shred your brie cheese before adding it to the mix.
6. You will need to mix everything really well because if you do not mix the Ingredients: everything will go out of proportion and it won't taste as good. You will then have to place the muffin holes inside the oven and bake them at 350 degrees for about 16 minutes.
7. When you get the muffin holes out of the oven you are done. You may want to use a sandwich bag in order to preserve this food.

8. This meal will last you for at least three days and you will not have to prepare the breakfast food every morning.
9. It is natural to assume that you can serve this meal with some vegetables and this is quite an important aspect. I like to serve this food with some chili and tomato.

Easy Chicken Curry

Ingredients:

- 250 grams of chicken
- 2 cloves of garlic
- 20 grams of curry spice
- 50 grams of tomatoes
- 100 grams of fat free yogurt
- 50 grams of onion
- 70 grams of cucumber
- 150 grams of mushrooms

Directions:

1. First of all you will have to chop all of your Ingredients: into similar sized pieces.

2. After you are done with chopping the Ingredients: you should place a pan on a low heat.
3. Lightly mist the pan with some low calorie cooking spray or olive oil.
4. After the pan has reached the boiling point you should add the onion and gently mix it for one minute.
5. After that you should add the cucumber and the chicken. Make sure to mix it really well before you finally add the garlic.
6. It is now time to add the tomatoes and curry spice. Make sure to stir fry all the Ingredients: for three minutes.
7. If you notice that the vegetables start to stick to the pan you should try to add a splash of water.
8. Towards the end of the cooking process you can add the mushrooms and keep on mixing

the Ingredients: until the mushrooms are nice and brown.
9. If you notice that the meat starts to form a yellow brown color than you should know that it is time to lift the pan from the heat and add some chopped tomatoes and stock.
10. Make sure to simmer for 30 minutes before finally lifting the pan. In the end you can two spoons of fat free yogurt.

Beef And Veggie Stirfry

Ingredients:

- 1 handful of snap peas
- 2 tablespoons coconut oil
- Salt and pepper to taste
- 2 cloves of garlic, minced
- 1 thumbsized piece of ginger, grated
- 1 Pound Of GrassFed Beef Strips
- 1 bell pepper, sliced
- 1 zucchini, sliced
- 2 tablespoons of tamari or coconut aminos

Directions:

1. Heat A Large Pan Or Wok Over MediumHigh Heat, Then Add The Coconut Oil.

2. Once the oil is hot, add the beef strips. Season with salt and pepper. Stirfry until the beef is browned, then remove from the pan and set aside.
3. In the same pan, add the sliced bell pepper, zucchini, and snap peas. Stirfry until they're tendercrisp.
4. Add the minced garlic and grated ginger to the pan, stir well.
5. Return the beef to the pan, add the tamari or coconut aminos, and stir everything together.
6. Serve the stirfry hot, as is or over a bed of cauliflower rice for a complete Bulletproof meal.
7. Remember, these recipes should be adjusted to your individual dietary needs and preferences. Enjoy your Bulletproof dinners!

Broccoli And Cauliflower Soup

Ingredients:

- 1 cup of broccoli florets
- 4 tbsp. of grassfed butter
- 1 cup of cauliflower florets
- sea salt (to taste)

Directions:

1. Add the half of the broccoli and cauliflower to the blender along with a cup of filtered water.
2. Start the blender of slow and gradually increase the speed. Add the rest of the Ingredients:.
3. Place the blended mixture in a saucepan and gently warm it up on a low heat.

Cauliflower Chowder Recipe

Ingredients:

- 4 cups of chicken stock

- 1 cup unsweetened coconut milk

- 1¼ tsp. ground cumin

- 1 tsp. ground turmeric

- ½ tsp. ground coriander

- 12 tbsp. grassfed butter or ghee

- 1 head of cauliflower, roughly chopped

- 4 slices of bacon, cooked and chopped

- 1 onion, diced

- 2 cloves of garlic, minced

- 2 stalks of celery, diced

- 2 carrots, peeled and chopped
- sea salt and freshly ground black pepper

Directions:

1. Melt the butter/ghee in a large saucepan placed over a medium heat.
2. Add the carrots, celery, onion, and garlic. Then cook the vegetables for about 5 minutes until tender.
3. Then stir in the chopped cauliflower and cook everything for a further 5 minutes, stirring occasionally.
4. Add the chicken stock, herbs, spices and coconut milk. Then stir everything together.
5. Bring to a boil. Then reduce the heat and let it simmer for about 15 minutes or until the vegetables are tender.
6. Season to taste, garnish with bacon and serve.

Beef Short Rib Soup

Ingredients:

- 2 Stalks of Celery, sliced

- 4 Carrots, sliced

- 3 Cloves of Garlic, minced

- Fresh Thyme, Tarragon and Sage, a few sprigs of each bundled together (If you only have dry versions available then just add a tsp. of each)

- 8 to 10 cups of water or Beef Stock

- 2 to 3 lbs. Beef Short Ribs

- 1.5 lbs. Beef Brisket, cubed

- 4 Leeks, sliced

- Sea salt and freshly ground black pepper

Directions:

1. Sear the beef in a Dutch oven over a high heat, this takes about 12 minutes per side.
2. Next, lower the heat and add the garlic, and cook until colored.
3. Then add the rest of the vegetables and the herb bundle (if you don't have the fresh herbs you can add the dry versions).
4. Top with water or beef stock and bring to a boil.
5. Lower the heat and simmer for 4 to 5 hours.
6. Remove the herb bundle, season to taste and serve.

Smoked Salmon Frittata

Ingredients:

For smoked salmon frittata:

- 8 large pasture eggs

- 1 tablespoon grass fed ghee or coconut oil

- 78 ounces smoked salmon

To serve:

- 1 green onion

- Green onion sauce as required

Directions:

Preheat the broiler.

1. Slice the green onion.
2. Add eggs to a bowl and beat the eggs with an electric mixer until light and fluffy. Set it aside.
3. Take an ovenproof skillet and place it over medium heat. Add ghee. When ghee melts,

add eggs and cook until the middle part is runny and sides are slightly set.
4. Place the smoked salmon on the eggs. Remove from heat.
5. Place the skillet under the broiler and cook until the eggs are set.
6. Remove from the oven. Garnish with green onions and serve with green onion sauce.

Bread

Ingredients:

- 2/3 cup apple sauce

- 12 pasture eggs

- 2/3 cup mct oil or coconut oil, melted

- 1 ½ cups coconut flour

- 1 teaspoon ground flax

- ½ teaspoon sea salt

Directions:
1. Add coconut flour, ground flax, applesauce, eggs, coconut oil to a bowl and stir. Using a hand blender, blend until smooth batter is formed.
2. Grease 2 small loaf pans and line with parchment paper.

3. Pour batter into the pans. Place the pans in an oven.
4. Bake in a preheated oven at 350 degree F for about 45 minutes.
5. Remove from oven and cool completely. Run a knife all around the edges of the bread and invert on to a plate.
6. Slice each loaf into 22 slices.
7. Fill with toppings of your choice and serve.

Winter Vegetable Salad

Ingredients:

- 1 small head cabbage, cored, cut long strips 1 inch width
- 1 teaspoon each of fresh rosemary, thyme and oregano chopped
- ¼ cup almonds, chopped
- 4 teaspoons apple cider vinegar
- 4 slices thick cut pastured bacon
- 12 teaspoons high quality olive oil
- 8 teaspoons bulletproof Brain Octane oil or MCT or coconut oil
- 1 pound each of parsnip, carrots, turnip, winter squash and sweet potatoes, chopped into 1 inch pieces

- Salt to taste

Directions:
1. Place bacon on a baking sheet that is lined with parchment paper. Bake in a preheated oven at 320 F for 10 minutes. Do not brown it. Only cook it.
2. Remove the bacon. When cool enough to handle, crumble and set aside.
3. Let the bacon fat remain on the baking sheet.
4. Add the vegetables to the baking sheet and pour Brain Octane oil, 8 teaspoons olive oil, salt, and fresh herbs. Toss well.
5. Bake for about 20 minutes.
6. Add cabbage and toss. Bake until vegetables are tender.
7. Remove from the oven and transfer into a large serving bowl. Pour the remaining oil over it. Sprinkle vinegar, bacon, and almonds and serve warm.

'Whatever' Stove Top Dinner

Ingredients:

- 1 'green zone' meat
- 12 'green zone' vegetables, chopped
- Spinach or kale
- Your choice herbs/spices

Directions:

1. Put some coconut oil in a pan on medium heat. Lightly brown the meat and then add the veggies and your leafy greens. Sprinkle in your spices and herbs.
2. Stir, cover, and let it cook until veggies are tender, usually 1015 minutes.

Creamy Broccoli Soup

Ingredients:

- 1 carrot, sliced
- 4 c bone broth or veggie broth
- ½ c grassfed butter
- 68 cups broccoli florets
- 34 shallots, minced
- Sea salt to taste

Directions:
1. Put a dab of butter into a large stockpot and lightly sauté the shallots and carrot.
2. Add the broccoli and cook until it's bright green. Pour in the broth and continue to cook until broccoli is tender.

3. Add the remaining butter and blend (a hand blender works well) until desired consistency. Season with sea salt and serve hot.

Lime Infused Steamed Broccoli

Ingredients:

- 1 tablespoon extra virgin coconut oil
- Juice of 1 organic lime
- 1 pound organic broccoli
- Pan of water for steaming broccoli

Directions:

1. Take water in a pan for boiling and set a steamer basket on top of it.
2. Chop broccoli into big florets. Discard the stalks.
3. Place the florets on the steamer basket and cook till the time broccoli turns bright green and becomes tender. This would take around 810 minutes.

4. Once broccoli is done take it out in a bowl and toss it with coconut oil and squeeze juice of half a lemon and serve immediately.

Icy Green Bulletproof Smoothie

Ingredients:

- 2 stick of organic celery
- 2 tablespoon organic apple cider vinegar
- Stevia as per taste
- 10 ounce of water
- 1 bunch organic romaine lettuce
- 1 an organic cucumber
- 2 organic green apple
- Cupful of crushed ice

Directions:

1. Wash and peel all vegetables and put them in a blender with water.
2. Blend it for about a minute and serve icy cold.

3. This is a refreshing summery drink with natural sweetness that you can enjoy guiltfree.

Shepherd's Pie

Ingredients:

- 2 c diced celery
- 2 lbs. ground beef
- 1 c bone or veggie broth
- 2 heads cauliflower
- ½ lb. bacon, chopped
- 2 c shredded carrots
- 1 c butter

Directions:
1. Cut and steam the cauliflower. Put it in a food processor or blender.
2. Add the butter and blend until nice and smooth. Set it aside.

3. Cook the bacon in a large fry pan, and then add the carrots and celery.
4. Continue cooking for about 5 minutes while you preheat the oven to 350 degrees F.
5. Add the ground beef to the fry pan along with a little salt and about half the broth.
6. Simmer and stir, adding more broth if it gets dry.
7. Cook until the broth has evaporated and the beef is cooked through. Spread the beef mixture in the bottom of a large baking dish with high sides.
8. Spoon the cauliflower on top and smooth. Bake uncovered for about 30 minutes until top starts to brown.

Cashewginger Butternut Soup

Ingredients:

- 6 carrots, chopped
- 1 c raw cashews, chopped
- 1inch piece fresh ginger, grated
- 2 tsp. ground cumin
- 1 large butternut squash
- 1 can (14 oz.) coconut milk
- 1 c bone broth or veggie stock
- 2 tsp. ground cinnamon

Directions:
1. Combine all Ingredients: and cook for 46 hours on low in a slow cooker or on the

stovetop on low heat, stirring regularly, for 23 hours.
2. Blend to a smooth consistency before serving.

Fresh Buttered Scallops

Ingredients:

- ¼ cup of tomato paste

- ¼ tsp. of cinnamon, ground

- 1 ½ tsp. of garam masala

- 8 ounces of coconut cream

- 1 pound of scallops, sea, fresh and cleaned

- dash of sea salt, for taste

- dash of pepper for taste

- dash of cayenne pepper for taste

- dash of cilantro, fresh and for garnish

- 2 tsp. of ginger, paste and fresh

- 2 tbsp. of coconut oil

- 2 tsp. of garlic, paste and fresh

- ½ cup of shallots, fresh and minced

- ¼ tsp. of cumin, ground

Directions:

1. Take out a large wok and heat up your coconut oil over medium to high heat.
2. Then add in your shallots and allow to cook for about 2 to 3 minutes or until the shallots begin to soften.
3. Next add in your tomato paste, ginger paste, garlic paste, garam masala, cumin, cayenne, cinnamon and season with salt and pepper.
4. Stir thoroughly to combine all of the Ingredients: together. All to cook for an additional 3 to 5 minutes, constantly stirring the entire time.
5. Add in your fresh scallops and your coconut cream to the pan and stir to combine everything.

6. Cook for another 5 minutes or until the scallops are fully cooked through.
7. Remove from heat and sprinkle your fresh cilantro on top of it all. Serve while still piping hot.

Creamy Tomato Soup

Ingredients:

- 2 liters of chicken stock, pastured

- 3 tsp. of basil, dried

- ½ tsp. of marjoram, dried

- 1 bay leaf

- 1/3 tsp. of thyme, dried

- ½ tsp. of oregano, dried

- ½ cup of tomatoes, fresh and diced

- 2 tbsp. of olive oil

- 2 tsp. of garlic, minced

- 1 cup of tomato paste

- dash of sea salt and pepper for taste

Directions:

1. Using a large sized skillet, sauté your onions over medium to high heat until the onions begin to turn translucent.
2. Then add in your garlic, tomatoes paste and cook for an additional 5 minutes.
3. Next add in your chicken stock, marjoram, thyme, basil, oregano, bay leaf and diced tomatoes. Bring this mixture to a rolling boil and then cook for an additional 30 minutes at low heat. Cover and let simmer.
4. Once fully cooked serve and enjoy while it is still piping hot.

Savory Beef Bake With Zucchini

Ingredients:

- 1 cup of celery, finely chopped
- 4 zucchini, sliced into ¼ inch slices
- some olive oil
- 1 tsp. of salt
- 1, 6 ounce can of tomato paste
- 1 cup of mushrooms, finely sliced
- ¼ tsp. of pepper
- ½ tsp. of oregano, dried
- 1 pound of beef, ground and grass fed
- 1 cup of onion, finely chopped
- 2 cups of mozzarella cheese, shredded

Directions:

1. Preheat your oven to 350 degrees. While your oven heats up place your zucchini onto a baking dish and arrange so that none of the zucchini are touching.
2. Then using a small sized skillet add in your onion, celery and oil. Sauté over medium to high heat for the next 5 minutes or until the onions begin to turn translucent.
3. Then add in your ground beef and cook until it is fully browned. Place you zucchini into the oven and allow to cook until the zucchini is fully tender. Remove from oven.
4. Pour your zucchini into your skillet and mix thoroughly with your ground beef mixture. Remove from heat and serve immediately.

PERFECT PARCHMENTBAKED SALMON

Ingredients:

- 1 tablespoon minced fresh herbs (such as chives, parsley, or dill)
- Lemon wedges, for serving
- 2 centercut wild salmon fillets (8 ounces each)
- 1 teaspoon Bulletproof Brain Octane oil (or MCT or coconut oil)
- Sea salt
- 1 tablespoon grassfed unsalted butter

Directions:
1. Preheat the oven to 320°F.
2. Place the salmon on a piece of parchment paper on a baking sheet.
3. Rub the fillets with Brain Octane oil, season with sea salt, and top with the butter. Wrap

the parchment around the fish, folding seams and tucking them to ensure steam does not escape.
4. Bake until fish is mediumrare, about 18 minutes. Sprinkle with the herbs and a squeeze of lemon.

GRILLED SALMON AND ZUCCHINI

Ingredients:

- 4 tablespoons fresh lemon juice
- 4 teaspoons highquality olive oil
- Sea salt
- 2 skinon wild salmon fillets (8 ounces each), skin scored lightly
- 1 pound zucchini, cut into 1/2inch slices
- 2 tablespoons plus 2 teaspoons Bulletproof Brain Octane oil (or MCT or coconut oil) 2 teaspoons minced fresh oregano
- 4 teaspoons finely chopped fresh herbs (such as chive, parsley, or oregano)

Directions:

1. Heat a grill pan over (or fire up your grill to) mediumhigh heat.
2. In a medium bowl, toss the zucchini with 2 tablespoons of the Brain
3. Octane oil. Grill lightly, in batches, reducing the heat or flame to low and turning halfway, until the zucchini is crisptender, 6 to 8 minutes.
4. Set the grill pan aside (or leave the grill on). Sprinkle the zucchini with the oregano, 2 tablespoons of the lemon juice, the olive oil, and sea salt to taste. Set aside.
5. If using a grill pan, heat over mediumhigh heat. Rub the salmon with the remaining 2 teaspoons Brain Octane oil and sprinkle with sea salt.
6. Place the salmon on the grill surface, skinsidedown, and cook about 6 minutes, reducing the heat to mediumlow as needed to avoid charring the skin.

7. Carefully flip the fillets and cook until fish is mediumrare, about 3 minutes longer.
8. Top the fish with herbs and the remaining 2 tablespoons lemon juice. Season to taste with sea salt and serve with the zucchini.

Baked Burgers

Ingredients:

- 2 t dried oregano
- sea salt (to taste)
- 4 slices bacon
- 2 lbs. ground beef (if not grassfed, use lean)
- 2 tsp. ground turmeric
- 1 t dried rosemary

Directions:

1. Preheat oven to 325 degrees F. Make about 8 burgers. Combine the spices and rub them directly onto the burgers. Salt to taste.
2. Put a halfslice of bacon on top of each burger and put them on a flat baking pan with sides. Bake for 1520 minutes to desired doneness.

Creamy Cauliflower

Ingredients:

- ½ head of cauliflower, broken into flowerets
- 3 t grassfed butter
- 2 t coconut oil, melted
- ½ tsp. apple cider vinegar
- your herbs of choice
- sea salt (to taste)

Directions:

1. Steam the cauliflower until tender. Put about twothirds into serving bowl andthe remaining third into a blender (or bowl if using a hand blender).

2. Add the remaining Ingredients: and blend until smooth. Pour the blended mixture backover the cauliflower in the serving bowl.

Beef Carpaccio, Hazelnuts & Egg Yolk Dressing

Ingredients:

- Tablespoon apple cider vinegar
- 1 teaspoon honey
- ½ cup rocket leaves
- Salt and pepper to taste
- 2 pounds of grass fed beef fillet
- ¼ cup hazelnuts, crushed
- 2 pastored egg yolks
- 6 tablespoon virgin olive oil

Directions:

1. Slice the fillet of beef into thin slices and bat out between two sheets of cling film.
2. Lay the beef so it covers the whole plate.

3. In a bowl add the egg yolk and slowly whisk in the oil to emulsify. Add the honey vinegar and salt and pepper.
4. To serve sprinkle the hazel nuts and rocket leaves over the beef and drizzle the dressing around the plate.

Trout And Avocado Lettuce Wraps

Ingredients:

- 2 scallions, finely chopped
- ¼ cup flat leaf parsley
- 4 tablespoon grass fed full fat yoghurt
- Salt and pepper to taste
- 2 fillets of trout
- 1 large avocado, peeled and cubed
- Juice of 1 lemon
- 1 head of baby gem lettuce

Directions:

1. Place the trout fillets in the bamboo steamer and cook for around 5 minutes.

2. In a bowl combine the avocado, scallions, parsley, yoghurt, lemon juice and salt & pepper. Flake the cooked trout into the bowl.
3. Mix well so the yoghurt coats all the Ingredients:.
4. Peel back the baby gem lettuce so you get small petal like cups.
5. Fill each cup with the filling and enjoy!

Red Onion Squash Soup

Ingredients:

- 1 sprig of fresh thyme
- 6 cups vegetable broth
- 1 cup organic grass fed cream
- ½ cup grass fed butter
- 1 pound red onion squash, peeled and cubed
- 2 onions, diced
- 2 clove garlic, sliced
- Salt and pepper to taste

Directions:

1. In a large sauce pan bring the butter to a medium heat.

2. Add the onion, garlic and thyme and cook gently for 10 minutes.
3. Add the squash and vegetable broth. Bring to the boil.
4. Cook for around 30 minutes.
5. Transfer to a liquidizer and blend until smooth.
6. Once smooth, add the cream, salt and pepper.
7. Serve hot!

Betterforyou Bulletproof Salad

Ingredients:

- ½ avocado, sliced

- ½ cup olives, sliced

- ½ cucumber, sliced thin

- 1 head of iceberg lettuce, chopped

- 1 handful of radishes, sliced thin

Directions:

1. Combine Ingredients: and toss. If desired, top with a bulletproof salad dressing recipe.

Avocado Dressing

Ingredients:

- 1 tablespoon lemon juice, freshly squeezed
- 1 cup cucumber, finely chopped
- ¼ cup cilantro, chopped
- ½ avocado, mashed
- 1 tablespoon apple cider vinegar
- 1 tablespoon MCT oil
- Sea salt, as desired

Directions:

1. Add all Ingredients: into your blender and use "medium" setting to reach your desired consistency. Incorporate with a bulletproof salad for a delicious and healthy lunch.

Guiltfree Ranch

Ingredients:

- 2 tablespoons fresh dill, finely chopped

- 1 tablespoon apple cider vinegar

- 1 cup Bulletproofapproved mayonnaise (made by combining 1 rawpastured egg with ¾ cups olive oil, ¼ cup MCT oil, and 2 teaspoons lemon juice)

- 2 garlic cloves, minced

- Sea salt

Directions:

1. Blend until smooth and refrigerate for 23 hours before serving with a bulletproof salad.

Bulletproof Steak Bowl

Ingredients:

- 1 tablespoons sea salt

- 1 teaspoon each sage, oregano, thyme, parsley and rosemary, roughly chopped and mixed

- 2 tablespoon Brain Octane C8 MCT Oil, plus extra for drizzling

- 1 cup (dry) organic long grain white rice, rinsed

- 2 cups water

- Vegetables of your choice, steamed

- 1 ½ pounds grassfed tri tip steak

- 2 tablespoons extra virgin olive oil

- 1 tablespoon grassfed butter

Directions:

1. Preheat oven to 350 degrees F.
2. Add rice, water, 1 teaspoon sea salt, and 2 tablespoons Brain Octane C8 MCT Oil to a pot. Bring to a boil, cover, reduce heat to low and cook for 20 minutes.
3. While rice is cooking, trim the fat and skin off the tri tip with a sharp knife. Fat is good, but you want the tri tip to be tender and easy to eat.
4. Rub the tri tip with olive oil until coated, then toss in sea salt and herb mixture.
5. Spread the tri tip on a baking pan and bake until mediumrare, 1820 minutes.
6. Remove the tri tip from the oven and let it rest for 10 minutes.
7. When the rice is done cooking, remove it and let it rest for 10 minutes.

8. Put the rice in the bottom of a bowl and top with steamed veggies, tri tip, grassfed butter, and salt to taste. Drizzle extra Brain Octane oil if you'd like, then serve.

www.ingramcontent.com/pod-product-compliance
Lightning Source LLC
LaVergne TN
LVHW010223070526
838199LV00062B/4706